TOMATOES

A TRUE BOOK

by
Elaine Landau

Children's Press®
A Division of Grolier Publishing
New York London Hong Kong Sydney
Danbury, Connecticut

Varieties of tomatoes

Reading Consultant
Linda Cornwell
*Coordinator of School Quality
and Professional
Improvement, Indiana State
Teachers Association*

Author's Dedication
For Michael

**Visit Children's Press® on the
Internet at:
http://publishing.grolier.com**

Library of Congress Cataloging-in-Publication Data

Landau, Elaine.
Tomatoes / by Elaine Landau.
    p.   cm. — (A True Book)
  Includes bibliographical references (p.) and index.
  Summary: Examines the history, cultivation, and uses of tomatoes.
  ISBN 0-516-21028-9 (Lib. bdg.)   0-516-26773-6 (pbk.)
  1. Tomatoes—History—Juvenile literature. 2. Tomatoes—Juvenile
literature. [1. Tomatoes.] I. Title. II. Series.
SB349.L34 1999
635'.642—dc21   98-49387
                                                  CIP
                                                  AC

GROLIER
PUBLISHING

Contents

Tomatoes add color and nutrition to salads (above). Tomato soup (left) is a delicious part of a quick meal.

The Best Part of a Salad

Think of a salad. What's the best tasting and most colorful part of it? If you said a tomato, you are not alone. Countless people would agree with you.

There are over four thousand different kinds of tomatoes. And they aren't only found in salads. This plump, red, round vegetable is what makes tomato juice tasty. It is the basis of tomato soup. And how good would a bacon, lettuce, and tomato sandwich be without the tomato? Tomatoes are used in many other ways, as well. The average American eats about 17 pounds (8 kilograms) of tomatoes a year. Tomatoes are also one of the most widely grown vegetable crops.

An American Vegetable

Tomatoes got their start in the highlands of South America. There, tomatoes grew wild in the Andes Mountains in what is now Peru, Ecuador, Colombia, and Chile. These wild tomatoes were not the average tomatoes you might find in your vegetable garden or supermarket.

Tiny cherry tomatoes (above) might be found growing wild in wooded areas. A sixteenth-century Peruvian Indian (left)

Instead, they looked like the small, round cherry tomatoes eaten today. Most were only about an inch (2.5 centimeters) wide.

The Inca Indians of Peru developed an advanced culture, but they showed little interest in the tomato. They may have picked them sometimes, but there wasn't even a name for the tomato in their language.

Later, wild tomatoes were found in parts of Central America and Mexico. Their tiny seeds had been carried there by strong winds, as well as on the fur of animals and feathers of birds heading north. It was here that people first came to value and enjoy the tomato.

The Indians living in these regions grew tomatoes as a crop. The Aztec Indians of Mexico had a highly developed civilization. They made many advances in agriculture, including ways to improve the tomato. They were careful to plant only the seeds from the biggest and best-tasting ones. They produced a fairly large tomato

Aztec ruler
Montezuma II
being carried
by his subjects
in a procession

that was yellowish in color.
When the first European con-
querors invaded the region,
they called it the golden apple.

Crossing the Atlantic

The Spanish conqueror Hernando Cortés and his soldiers invaded Mexico in 1521. When they returned to Spain they brought back many items from the Americas. The golden apple, or tomato as we know it, was among these.

Before long, the tomato was taken to Italy and other parts of Europe. At that time, tomatoes weren't eaten raw. Instead, they were cut into pieces, seasoned with salt and pepper, and fried in oil.

Yellow pear tomatoes (above)
and tree tomatoes (right)

By the late 1500s tomatoes
were grown in home gardens in
England, Germany, Belgium,
and France. Some of these varieties (types) were yellow while
others were red. In France the

14

tomato was known as the love apple rather than the golden apple. People believed that tomatoes caused those who ate them to fall in love.

At first, the tomato wasn't widely accepted. Many people refused to eat them. It wasn't that they disliked the flavor. But in the early 1500s it was rumored that tomatoes weren't safe to eat.

That's because botanists (scientists who study plant life) learned that the tomato was a

The black nightshade plant, with flower and fruit

member of the nightshade family. Some plants in this family are poisonous. And even though the tomato plant's leaves and stems are mildly poisonous— the tomato itself is completely safe. Yet, for many years the tomato was not usually found on the dinner table.

Instead, bright red tomatoes were grown to add a delightful splash of color in gardens. Tomatoes were also planted over arbors and in fancy pots as decorations.

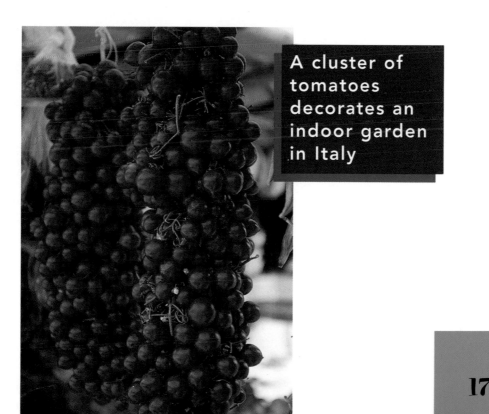

A cluster of tomatoes decorates an indoor garden in Italy

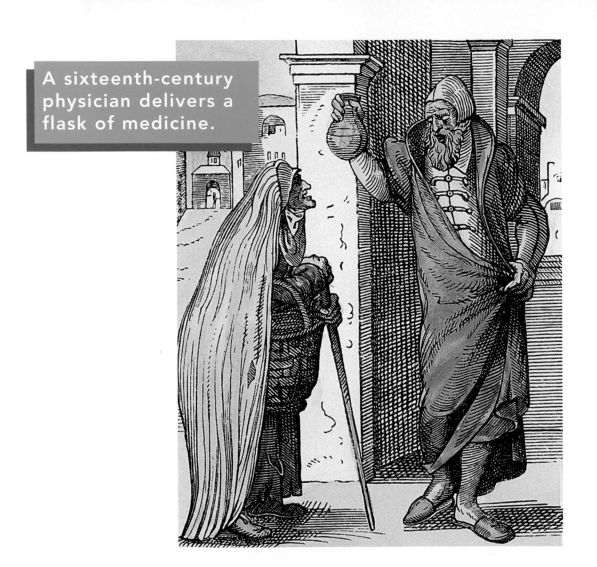

A sixteenth-century physician delivers a flask of medicine.

The tomato was also some-
times used as a medicine.
European healers rubbed the

liquid from its stems and leaves on various skin conditions. Surprisingly, in the 1940s scientists learned that this fluid actually helps fight certain types of fungi.

There were other medical claims about the healing powers of the tomato. At different times, tomato juice was said to cure upset stomachs, sore throats, and even blindness. However, there was no truth to these claims.

Back to America

When Europeans came to the colonies in North America, they brought tomato plants with them. Unfortunately, they brought their mistaken ideas about the vegetable as well. Often, these plants continued to be grown mainly as decorations.

Thomas Jefferson (left) was an avid gardener at his Virginia estate, Monticello.

Thomas Jefferson, the third president of the United States, planted tomatoes in his garden. And the vegetable was sometimes sold in food markets. But for the most part, only the French settlers in New Orleans purchased them. They used tomatoes to make ketchup.

In time, tomatoes became more accepted as a food. A man named Robert Gibbon Johnson, from the small village of Salem, New Jersey, is often given credit for this. According to the story, Johnson grew tomatoes and enjoyed eating them. He had urged surrounding farmers to grow tomato crops, but they refused. So Johnson became determined to prove that tomatoes were both safe and delicious.

He announced that he would eat several tomatoes on the steps of the village hall in front of anyone who cared to watch. And on a sunny after-noon in 1820 he did just that, to the amazement of a crowd of townspeople.

While this story has often been told, it's doubtful that Johnson had any real effect on tomato sales. Yet at about the same time, tomatoes were beginning to become more accepted than in the past. New, better-tasting varieties had been developed. In addition, improved cross-country transportation had made it easier to ship these vegetables long distances.

The Tomato Business

By the late 1800s, tomatoes had reached new heights. Having planted seeds from only the tastiest samples, growers produced a smooth, red tomato with a sweet, tangy flavor. Farmers grew large quantities of the vegetable and shipped their

produce to markets in surrounding areas.

Some of the larger growers set up factories to can tomatoes. These included Joseph Campbell, whose cannery later became the Campbell Soup Company. Before long, tomatoes were processed for a variety of uses. People were finally ready to buy tomato juice, tomato sauce, tomato ketchup, tomato soup, and other tomato-based products.

FROM THE SUN-DRENCHED FIELDS OF SUMMER

Luscious, specially grown tomatoes make
"The Soup Most Folks Like Best"

Remember how they looked—those sun-bathed fields?
The rich dark loam, the rows of lush green-growing plants,
the peeping deep-red tomatoes fairly bursting with juice
and goodness? Such are the prize tomatoes used in making
Campbell's Tomato Soup.

Sit down soon to a plate of this favorite soup of all.
You'll revel in the flavor of those specially grown tomatoes
made into a smooth purée, with golden table butter and a
whisper of seasoning—all according to a matchless recipe.
Prepare it with milk, sometimes, instead of water, for an
extra-delicious cream of tomato. Have it soon!

Campbell's TOMATO SOUP

Campbell's Tomato Soup, introduced in 1897, was one of the products invented at Joseph Campbell's New Jersey cannery.

In the 1890s, a serious debate arose over whether the tomato was a fruit or a vegetable. Botanists said the tomato was a fruit because of its fleshy pulp, seeds, and other fruitlike traits. But for financial reasons, it was very important to United States tomato growers that it be considered a vegetable.

That's because all vegetables coming into the United States at that time from other

A sliced tomato shows the properties it shares with other fruits.

countries were taxed. However, fruits were not. With the tomato considered a fruit, large quantities of them were shipped to the United States from Cuba and

Mexico. This seriously cut into the market United States farmers felt was theirs.

If the tomato were a vegetable, the situation would change. The tax would force foreign growers to price their tomatoes higher, giving United States growers more power in the marketplace.

The question was brought before the United States Supreme Court. And in 1893, to the home growers' delight, the Court ruled that tomatoes were vegetables. It based its decision on how the tomato was used. Tomatoes were usually eaten in salads or with meals like many other vegetables. Unlike fruits, tomatoes generally weren't eaten as snacks or in pies, cakes, or ice cream.

The victory meant far greater profits for United States tomato growers. Their business boomed.

One Tomato, Two Tomato

Tomatoes and tomato sauce make this easy pizza recipe twice as good for an after-school snack.

Pizza Bagels

You will need:

- Tomato sauce (or pizza sauce)
- mozzarella cheese, shredded
- tomatoes, sliced or chopped
- pepperoni, if desired
- bagels, cut in half

With an adult's help, shred the cheese, cut up the tomatoes, and slice the bagels in half. Spread tomato sauce over each bagel. Arrange tomatoes and pepperoni slices on the sauce, and then sprinkle with the shredded cheese. Cook in the microwave for 30 seconds on high, checking to see if more or less time is needed. The pepperoni should be sizzling and the cheese melted. Let it cool a bit before digging in!

Tomatoes, Tomatoes, Tomatoes

Today, more tomatoes are grown in the United States than anywhere else in the world. Tomatoes do best in fertile, well-drained soil. They also need a warm climate. Therefore, tomatoes are mostly grown in California, Florida,

Tomatoes in this greenhouse are grown hydroponically, or without soil but with extra nutrients.

and other warm areas during the winter. They are grown in cooler regions in the summer. Tomatoes are also grown in greenhouses.

Tomatoes are often shipped long distances to markets. To

prevent them from spoiling, they are picked before they are fully ripe. Some tomatoes are picked by hand, others by machines. Either way, when they reach their destination, they are put in a warm room or warehouse to finish ripening. Then they are ready for you to buy.

The tomatoes used in various products, such as tomato soup, are picked when they've ripened. Often, the

Picking tomatoes in Ontario, Canada (above)
A tomato cannery in California (left)

processing plants they are sent to are nearby. They'll later be shipped out in cans, bottles, or other types of containers.

A Healthy Choice

Are tomatoes good for you? You bet they are! A single medium-size tomato provides about half of the recommended daily allowance of vitamin C. It also contains vitamin A. Some of this is in the form of beta-carotene, which doctors think reduces the risk of certain types of cancers.

Sun dried tomatoes are another popular tomato product.

Tomatoes are also a good source of potassium and contain some B vitamins, iron, and phosphorous. They are low in sodium and calories, and are cholesterol free. In addition, tomatoes are a rich source of fiber.

An outdoor street market in Boston

Knowing that tomatoes are good for you, you might want to eat more of them. Some people claim that homegrown tomatoes are best. Others are satisfied with the ones they buy in stores. But wherever you get your tomatoes, it's important to know how to select and keep them.

To choose a ripe tomato, check the vegetable's color. It should be a bright, shiny red. Check for firmness as well. A

With practice, you can pick the perfect tomato easily.

ripe tomato isn't rock hard. Pass up a tomato that shows any signs of decay as well. Remember that a fully ripened tomato should be eaten as soon as possible.

Tomatoes that have not completely ripened should be stored at room temperature. Be sure to keep them out of direct sunlight. You can speed up the ripening process by placing the tomato in a brown paper bag with a piece of fruit, such as a peach or pear.

But most importantly, never refrigerate a tomato that has not completely ripened. This destroys both its flavor and firmness.

Enjoy your tomatoes. They are good for you and delicious too.

To Find Out More

Here are some additional resources to help you learn more about tomatoes:

 **Books**

Kuhn, David. **More Than Just a Vegetable Garden.** Silver Press, 1990.

Moss, Miriam. **Fruit.** Garrett Educational Corp., 1993.

Nottridge, Rhoda. **Vitamins.** Carolrhoda Books, 1993.

Reed-King, Susan. **Food and Farming.** Thompson Learning, 1993.

Watts, Barrie. **Tomato.** Silver Burdett Press, 1989.

Organizations and Online Sites

California Sun Dry
901 Mariner's Island Blvd.
Suite 175
San Mateo, CA 94404
http://www.calsundry.com/Home.html

The sun dried tomato and salsa products company offers a photographic tour of the drying process, plus interesting facts and recipes.

The California Tomato Growers Association
10730 Siskiyou Lane
P.O. Box 7398
Stockton, CA 95267-0398
http://www.ctga.org/

This farmer-owned cooperative's site features Tomato Trivia, crop information, recipes, and links.

Campbell Soup Company
http://www.campbellsoup.com/

Homepage of the maker of Campbell's Tomato Soup. Visit Fun and Games Park, the Art of Soup Gallery, and click on Labels for Education to learn about the program. Also check out Campbell's Canada, in French or English.

Gardening and Growing Tomatoes
http://www.cyber-north.com/gardening/tomato.html

Clear diagrams and detailed instructions to help you grow the best tomatoes.

New Jersey Championship Tomato Weigh-In
http://www.njtomato.com/

Features "America's #1 Big Tomato Contest." Techniques for growing big tomatoes, health news, tomato recipe links, plus a picture gallery of contest finalists with their prize-winning tomatoes.

Important Words

arbor a structure used to support vines or trees

botanist a scientist who studies plant life

cannery a factory where foods are canned

debate to discuss or argue about

fungus a plant, such as a mold or a mushroom, that grows in dark, moist places (plural: fungi)

greenhouse a mostly glass building used for growing plants

nightshade a poisonous plant that has white flowers and black berries

pulp the moist, soft, fleshy part of a fruit

trait a special quality

varieties types or kinds

Index

Meet the Author

Elaine Landau worked as a newspaper reporter, an editor, and a youth services librarian before becoming a full-time writer. She has written more than one hundred nonfiction books for young people, including True Books on dinosaurs, animals, countries, and food.

Ms. Landau, who has a bachelor's degree from New York University and a master's degree in library and information science from Pratt Institute, lives in Florida with her husband and son.